Awesome
AMPHIBIANS

CREEPY CREATURES

Awesome
AMPHIBIANS

Written by Steve Parker

Scientific Consultant Joyce Pope
Illustrated by Ann Savage

RSVP
RAINTREE
Steck-Vaughn
P U B L I S H E R S
The Steck-Vaughn Company

Austin, Texas

Library of Congress Cataloging-in-Publication Data
Parker, Steve.
Awesome amphibians / written by Steve Parker.
p. cm. — (Creepy creatures)
Includes index.
Summary: Examines the physical characteristics, habitat, and behavior of various
frogs, toads, salamanders, and other denizens of the amphibian world.
ISBN 0-8114-0661-X
1. Amphibians—Juvenile literature. [1. Amphibians.]
I. Title. II. Series: Parker, Steve. Creepy creatures.
QL644.2.P37   1994
597.6—dc20   92-43196   CIP   AC

Editors: Wendy Madgwick, Susan Wilson
Designer: Janie Louise Hunt

Color reproduction by Global Colour, Malaysia
Printed by L.E.G.O., Vicenza, Italy
1 2 3 4 5 6 7 8 9 0 LE 98 97 96 95 94 93

Contents

Awesome Amphibians

Amphibians are animals that lead a strange double-life. They start life as eggs, black specks wrapped in a jelly coat. They develop into tadpoles, with frilly gills and wriggly tails, that live in water. Then they grow legs, lose their tails, leave the water, and hop onto the land as adult amphibians. These changes in form are known as metamorphosis.

eggs

tadpoles

▶ The **European frog** shows the typical frog features. Its big eyes watch out for prey and danger, its wide mouth gulps down its food, and its short body, small front legs, and very strong back legs are helpful for leaping and swimming. It has no tail.

▼ Amphibian tadpoles are usually smaller than the adults. But the tadpole of the **paradoxical frog**, from South America, grows bigger than its parent. As it becomes an adult, it shrinks!

▲ Most amphibians lay their eggs in water. But the **midwife toad** carries its eggs wrapped around its back legs. And the mid-"wife" is really the father! He dips the eggs in puddles to keep them damp. When the tadpoles hatch, he lets them swim away into the pond.

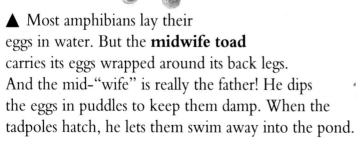

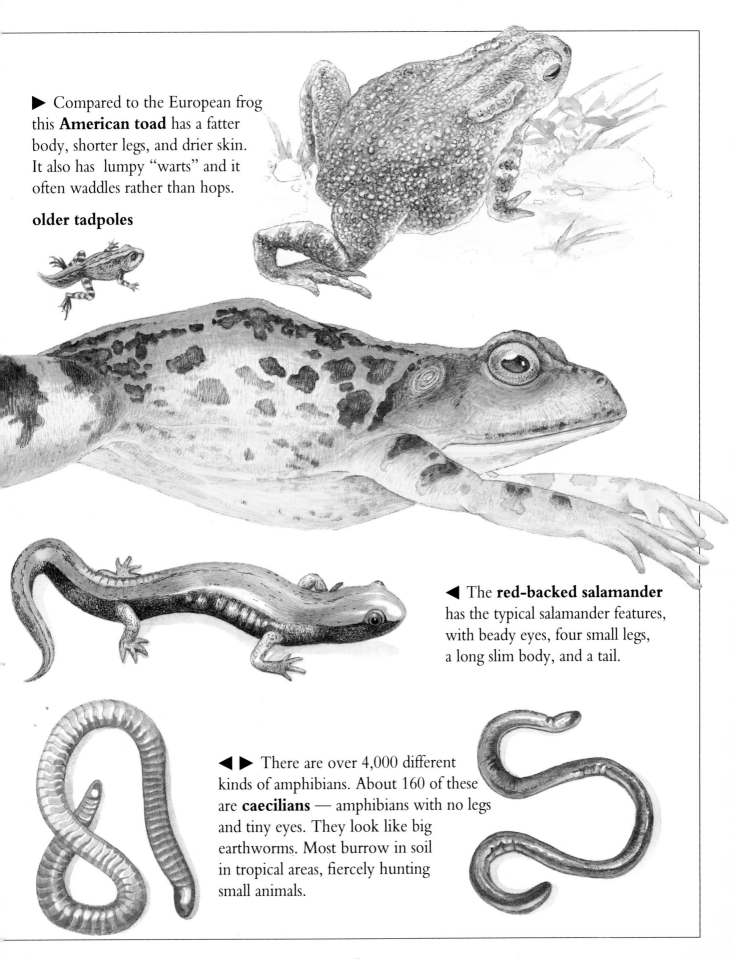

▶ Compared to the European frog this **American toad** has a fatter body, shorter legs, and drier skin. It also has lumpy "warts" and it often waddles rather than hops.

older tadpoles

◀ The **red-backed salamander** has the typical salamander features, with beady eyes, four small legs, a long slim body, and a tail.

◀▶ There are over 4,000 different kinds of amphibians. About 160 of these are **caecilians** — amphibians with no legs and tiny eyes. They look like big earthworms. Most burrow in soil in tropical areas, fiercely hunting small animals.

Frightful Frogs

Frogs turn up in all kinds of stories and legends. Sometimes they are evil creatures that hide in the dark and damp. Fairytale frogs turn into handsome princes when they are kissed. Frogs may look frightful, but they are more fascinating than frightening. They live in swamps and streams, on mountains, in caves, in deserts — almost everywhere, except the cold poles of the earth and the ocean.

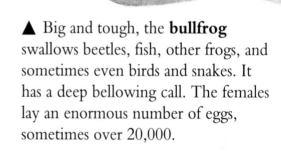

▲ Big and tough, the **bullfrog** swallows beetles, fish, other frogs, and sometimes even birds and snakes. It has a deep bellowing call. The females lay an enormous number of eggs, sometimes over 20,000.

▲ Most frogs live in damp places, which helps keep their skin moist. This is necessary because frogs breathe through their skin, as well as through their lungs. But the **water-holding frog** lives in Australian deserts and survives drought in its own underwater pond. This is formed by a water-filled "jacket" inside its outer layer of skin.

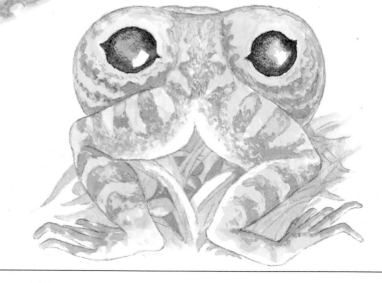

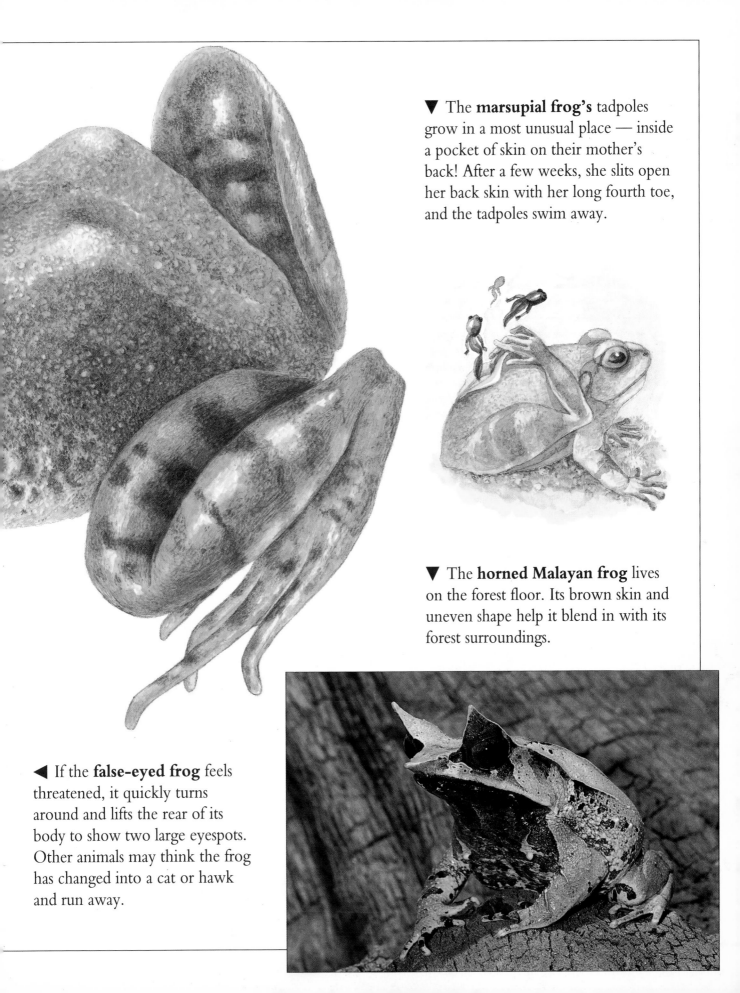

▼ The **marsupial frog's** tadpoles grow in a most unusual place — inside a pocket of skin on their mother's back! After a few weeks, she slits open her back skin with her long fourth toe, and the tadpoles swim away.

▼ The **horned Malayan frog** lives on the forest floor. Its brown skin and uneven shape help it blend in with its forest surroundings.

◄ If the **false-eyed frog** feels threatened, it quickly turns around and lifts the rear of its body to show two large eyespots. Other animals may think the frog has changed into a cat or hawk and run away.

Find the Frog!

Most frogs are not active hunters, chasing after their prey. Instead, they use ambush tactics. They sit and wait in a likely place for a meal in the shape of a worm, fly, or slug, to wander past. The frogs' pattern and coloring help to conceal and camouflage these quiet hunters in their natural surroundings.

► The **European tree frog** spends nearly all its time in trees, hiding in the leaves or crouching on the green stems. Its tongue flicks out to capture small insects in midflight.

▲ The **barred leaf frog** lives in the Amazon jungle. With its legs folded against its green body, the frog is hard to see among the leaves.

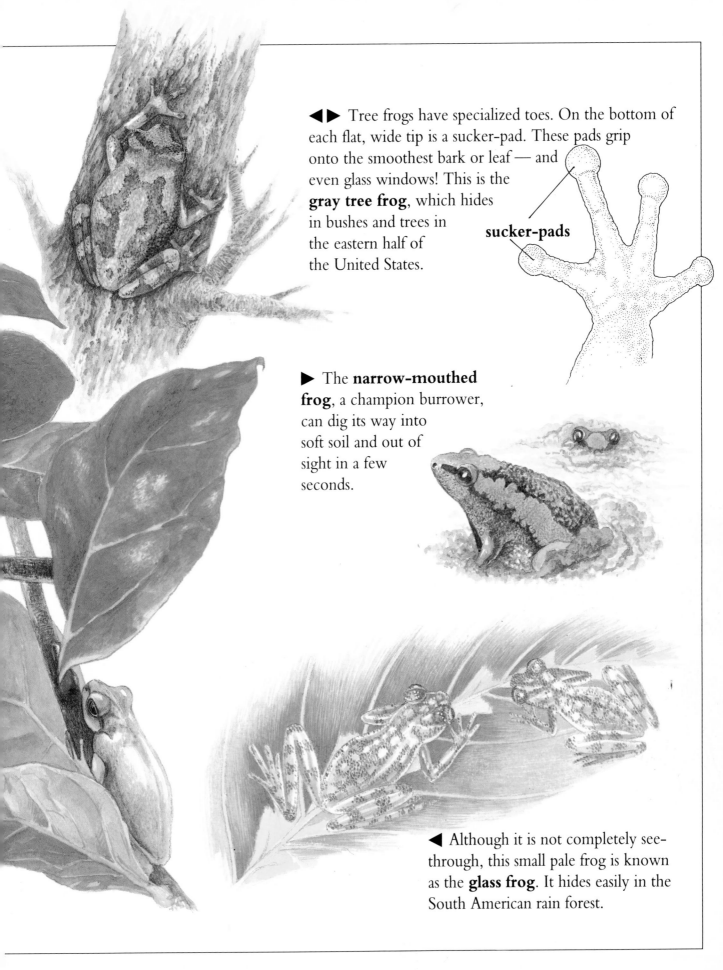

◀▶ Tree frogs have specialized toes. On the bottom of each flat, wide tip is a sucker-pad. These pads grip onto the smoothest bark or leaf — and even glass windows! This is the **gray tree frog**, which hides in bushes and trees in the eastern half of the United States.

sucker-pads

▶ The **narrow-mouthed frog**, a champion burrower, can dig its way into soft soil and out of sight in a few seconds.

◀ Although it is not completely see-through, this small pale frog is known as the **glass frog**. It hides easily in the South American rain forest.

Fearsome Frogs

It is wise to be fearful of certain frogs. If you touch them, the poisons in their skin could give you a skin rash and make you ill. The frog's bright colors and vivid patterns warn other animals about the poison. Any creature foolish enough to ignore the warning and eat one of these frogs, would probably die.

▼ In South America, local Indians tip their arrows with poisons from the skins of several kinds of frogs. So the frogs are called poison-arrow or arrow-poison frogs. The **golden poison-arrow frogs** are small and fierce — they fight each other at breeding time.

dart poison-arrow frog

kokoi poison-arrow frog

▶ Many of the poisonous frogs like this red-and-blue **poison-arrow frog** carry their developing tadpoles on their backs. The tadpoles are not in danger of drying out in the damp, steamy tropical rain forest.

▼ The **kokoi poison-arrow frog** from Colombia is one of the deadliest of all frogs. The poison from the skin of one of these tiny frogs could be used to kill dozens of people.

▼ Yellow-and-black markings are common warning colors in nature found in many bees, wasps, and snakes. Black and yellow also warn of skin poisons in the **harlequin frog**.

dart poison-arrow frog

▼ The **corroboree frog** from Australia looks as if it's advertising its poisonous skin. Yet it is not particularly poisonous. Its bright markings help protect it from predators.

Frog Songs

Why do frogs sing? Males sing to attract females at breeding time. At a busy pool in the spring dusk, their croaks and calls and squeaks and cheeps may seem like a deafening din to our ears. But each female frog can detect a male of her own kind from his song. She follows the sound and soon finds her way to him, even in the dark.

▼ In the eastern United States, the bell-like calls of **spring peepers** are a familiar sound as the snow and ice thaw. These common frogs hunt on the ground and in trees.

▲ One of the noisiest singers is the **marsh frog** of Europe. It calls throughout the year, and all night and day during the breeding season. The balloons of skin in its cheeks, called vocal sacs, make the noise even louder.

◄ In parts of Texas, ponds and pools echo to the sound of — bleating sheep? In fact, it's the male **sheep frog** making his mating call to attract females and warn off other males.

▼ The **painted reed frog** blows up his chin so much as he trills that it's bigger than his body!

▼ The **cricket frog** is named from its springtime song, which sounds like the harsh buzz of a cricket or grasshopper. It is only an inch long.

▶ Although it is called the **bell frog**, this creature's call sounds more like someone sawing wood! It stays mainly in lakes and large pools, and may eat its own tadpoles.

Famous Frogs

Frogs have become famous for various reasons. Some have strange breeding methods. Others are very rare and protected by laws. A few frogs are caught and kept as pets. This is usually regrettable because the frogs are taken from the wild, and so they become rarer, and even more valuable, and this makes them even more famous … and so the cycle goes on.

▶ One of the most unusual frogs in the world is the **Conondale gastric-brooding frog** from Australia. The mother swallows her own eggs, and the tadpoles grow inside her stomach! She cannot feed for several weeks, until she spits up the tiny froglets.

▲ The **tailed frog** from hillside streams in parts of the Pacific northwest can wag its fleshy "tail." Only males have tails, which they use when mating to fertilize the female's eggs.

▶ The tadpoles of **Darwin's frog**, from South America, live in their father's mouth! When the tadpoles develop into young frogs, the adult male frog opens its mouth wide, and the froglets jump out and swim off.

▼ Baby kangaroos and opossums grow inside a pouch on their mother's body. In a similar way, tadpoles of the **pouched frog** live in two pockets of skin on their father's body, giving this frog another name — the **hip-pocket frog**.

▼ **Hochstetter's frog** from New Zealand is rare, and the hill and mountain areas where it lives are preserved by law. It lays its eggs under stones or old logs. The tadpoles develop inside the eggs and hatch out as baby frogs 40 days later.

▼ The champion jumper of the frog world is the **African sharp-nosed frog**. It can hop over 17 feet (5.2m). If it were as big as a human, this would be equal to a long jump of 500 feet (150m)!

Feeding and Flying Frogs

All amphibians are hunters. They prey on other animals, which they often swallow whole — and still alive! Many frogs are not choosy about their victims. They eat snails, slugs, worms, beetles, flies, moths, spiders, fish … in fact, anything that fits into their wide-open mouths.

▶ Most frogs, like this **European frog**, hunt mainly by sight. Amphibians that live in murky water, or in caves, use their senses of smell and touch.

1. As it watches a fly buzzing past, the frog's brain works out the speed and direction in a split second, like a tiny computer.

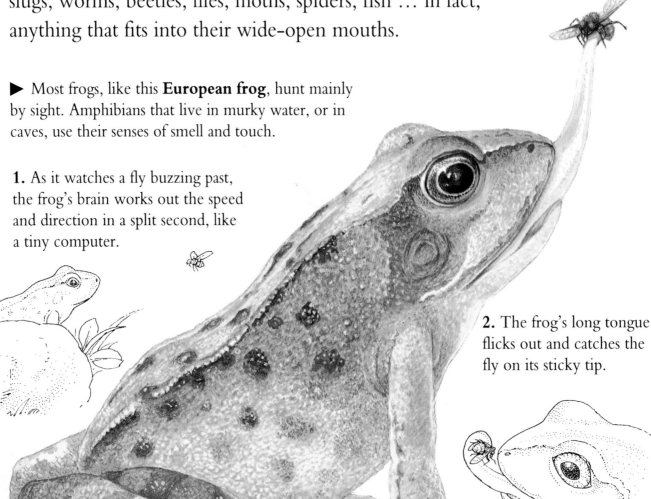

2. The frog's long tongue flicks out and catches the fly on its sticky tip.

3. The tongue curls back into the frog's mouth, which snaps shut on its prey — all in the blink of an eye.

▶ The strong **South African bullfrog** lunges at its prey of lizards, mice, fish, and other frogs, stuffing them into its mouth with its front feet.

◀ **Wallace's flying frog** cannot truly fly, but it does swoop from one tree to another, chiefly to escape enemies. This amazing amphibian, from the rain forests of Southeast Asia, glides using its huge feet. It stretches out the webbed skin between its toes like four tiny parachutes.

▶ Looking like a dead leaf on the forest floor of Central America, the **casque-headed frog** waits patiently. Sooner or later, an unwary snail or insect will wander past and — snap, it will be gone.

Terrifying Toads

"Eye of newt and tongue of toad …"
Many witches' spells feature lumpy, warty
toads, with their squinty eyes and tubby
bodies. True, most toads live in cool, damp
places, where they hide in the gloom.
But this is not because they are bewitched!
If a toad gets too dry or warm, its skin dries
out completely, and it dies.

**African clawed
toad swimming**

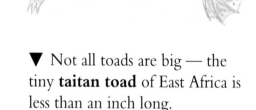

▼ Not all toads are big — the
tiny **taitan toad** of East Africa is
less than an inch long.

▲ A toad's skin, as on this **European
toad**, is usually lumpy and warty.
Tiny glands in its skin produce
unpleasant or poisonous fluids.

◀ The **African clawed toad** uses sharp claws on its front feet to feel in the mud for worms, water snails, and other food. It is an expert swimmer and, surprisingly for a toad, spends most of its life in water.

▲ Like most toads, the **southern toad** from the southeast of the United States has a bulge, the parotid gland, behind each eye. This makes a horrible-tasting or even poisonous fluid that protects the toad from being eaten.

▶ After she has laid her eggs, the female **Surinam toad** collects them on her back, and her skin grows over them. The tadpoles develop inside these "backpacks." They pop out three months later as fully formed tiny toads!

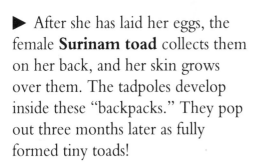

Tenacious Toads

Toads tend to be slow, but stubborn, or tenacious. Once they have got their mouths around their prey, they are unlikely to let go. Neither the slimy mucus produced by a trapped slug, nor the poisonous bite of a snared spider, nor the sharp kicks of a captured grasshopper make the toad loosen its grip. It slowly squashes life out of its victim with its mouth, jaws, and tongue.

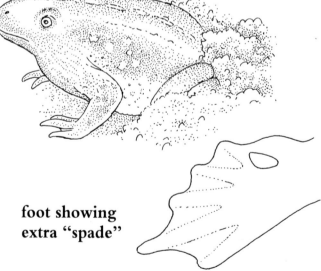

▼ With a mouth that seems wider than its head, the **Surinam horned toad** is a tough beast of the tropical woodland in northern South America. Its prey includes lizards and snakes, and other frogs and toads. It overcomes them with repeated bites, and swallows them whole.

foot showing extra "spade"

▲ As soon as the **Mexican burrowing toad** senses danger, it digs back-feet-first into the soil. The first toe on each foot is shovel-shaped, and there is also an extra bony "spade" next to this toe.

▼ This is a **giant toad**. No, it's a **marine toad**. No, it's a **cane toad**! In fact, it's all three. This big amphibian, up to 10 inches (25cm) long, comes from Central and South America. The fluid from its poison glands could kill a predator as large as a dog.

▲ This **African toad** belongs to the bufonids, the largest group of "typical" toads. There are more than 200 different species and they are found worldwide.

▼ The **Surinam toad** spends nearly all its life in water. It feels for food in the murky, muddy bottom using its long, sensitive toes. It also eats dead, rotting creatures — most unusual for a toad! The female carries her young on her back.

▲ In Australia the marine toad is called a **cane toad** because it was introduced into sugarcane fields to eat insect pests. But the toad settled in too well, and now it's a pest itself!

Tranquil Toads

If you happen upon a toad, it may slowly turn and walk away. Or it may simply sit and wait. Toads are well protected by the poison glands in their skin, which make awful-tasting, stinging, and even deadly fluids. Not many enemies tackle a toad twice. The fluids are especially effective if they get into the mouth of the predator. Some toads have other ways to protect themselves.

▼ As in other poison-arrow frogs, the bright colors of **Boulenger's poison-arrow toad** warn of the very poisonous fluids in its skin.

topside

► The **western spadefoot toad** found mainly in Arizona and New Mexico takes up a typical toad defense pose when it faces danger. It puffs itself up, hisses, and raises its rear to show off its lumpy skin and parotid glands.

◄ The **fire-bellied toad** does not look too scary. Its mottled greenish black skin gives good camouflage. But get too close, and it does a backflip to show off its bright red underside. That's much more frightening! If that doesn't work, its skin oozes a white fluid which stings the predator's mouth, nose, and eyes.

underside

▲ Looking like a burned cinder, **Nicholl's toadlet** is black all over. When attacked, this Australian toad lowers its head and fakes death, hoping its enemy will lose interest.

► When fall comes in the East, the **American toad** digs a burrow up to 3 feet (1m) deep in the soil. Here it sleeps until spring. If disturbed during winter, it may not move — not because it's afraid, but because its body is too cold.

Tough Toads

Most amphibians live in watery or damp places, but toads have spread and adapted to dry regions, even scrublands and deserts. This is because their thick, rough skin is good at keeping in body moisture. Also, most of them are active at night, when even the desert air can be cool.

▼ **Natterjack toads** prefer sandy scrublands and dunes by the coast. They dig their burrows with their front legs, throwing the sand behind them like a dog.

◄ With the first rains of summer this **giant African bullfrog** (about 7 inches or 18cm long) emerges from hibernation in its wintertime burrow. Its West African cousin, the goliath frog, is even larger at up to 14 inches (36 cm)!

▼ The **red-spotted toad**, which lives in the desert-like southwest, avoids the heat and dryness of the day by hiding in a burrow, or under logs and stones. At night it hunts beetles, crickets, and other small creatures.

▲ In a small area of Western Australia, **sand-dune frogs** live in — sand dunes! They burrow head-first, pushing away the sand with their snouts and front legs.

▶ The **green toad** can survive in dry sandy and grassy places and can even exist in slightly brackish (partly salty) water. It has spread across Europe, North Africa, and Central Asia.

Slinky Salamanders

Newts and mudpuppies, as well as various salamanders, all belong to a group of animals known as salamanders. There are about 350 kinds, or species, in this group. In general, salamanders have a long body and tail and four short legs. Like frogs and toads, salamanders are hungry predators, and many have poisons in their skin.

▲ The **tiger salamander**, which makes its home in most parts of the United States, is the largest land-living salamander. It grows up to 16 inches (40cm) long — big enough to eat mice and frogs.

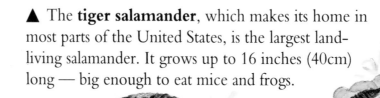

▶ According to legend, **fire salamanders** can walk through flames. Truly, they can't! The story may have come about when people collected old, damp logs to put on the fire. Salamanders hiding in the logs soon came running out!

▼ The **Asian giant salamander** is not only the biggest salamander, it's also the biggest amphibian. It grows up to 5 feet (1.5m) long. Its huge mouth easily swallows fish and crayfish.

greater siren in damp mud

► An eel-like salamander with tiny front legs but no hind legs, the **greater siren** lives in Florida and the surrounding states. If its swamp dries out, it makes a slimy casing around itself in the damp mud, and waits for rain.

► Like frogs, female salamanders lay jelly-covered eggs in water or in a damp place on land. The eggs develop into tadpole-like larvae and then into small adults. The **red-backed salamander** lays her eggs under a stone or old log and guards them.

eggs

adult

tadpoles

Surprising Salamanders

Some types of salamanders are most unusual. A few look as if they have never grown up. They still keep the red, feathery, blood-filled gills that all salamander larvae have when they are young. Most salamanders "breathe" in oxygen through their lungs and skin. The gills help them to take in extra oxygen, which is in short supply in warm, still waters.

▲ Unlike frogs and toads, most salamanders do not make sounds. But the **Pacific giant salamander** sings a low cry or howl. Its growing larva are sometimes cannibals — they eat their smaller brothers and sisters.

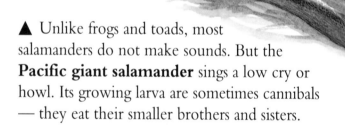

◄ **Congo-eels** or **amphiumas** are unusual salamanders found in the Carolinas and through most of the South, in swamps and ditches. Their legs are so surprisingly small, they seem to be useless for walking.

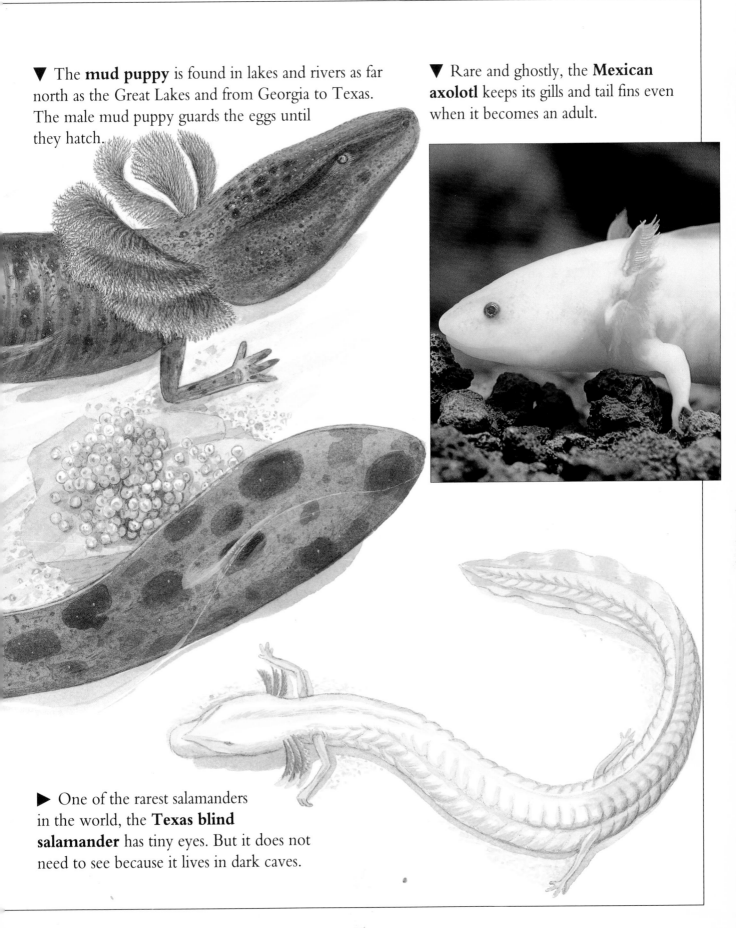

▼ The **mud puppy** is found in lakes and rivers as far north as the Great Lakes and from Georgia to Texas. The male mud puppy guards the eggs until they hatch.

▼ Rare and ghostly, the **Mexican axolotl** keeps its gills and tail fins even when it becomes an adult.

▶ One of the rarest salamanders in the world, the **Texas blind salamander** has tiny eyes. But it does not need to see because it lives in dark caves.

Nasty Newts

Newts can be very nasty, but only when animals such as birds, snakes, and fish try to eat them. Like other amphibians, they can ooze horrible-tasting or poisonous fluid from their skin. Normally newts are helpful to people because they eat garden pests such as slugs and flies.

non-breeding male

breeding male

female

▲ The **smooth newt** may look cute and even cuddly, but it is a greedy feeder. It grabs and gulps down all kinds of small creatures, from snails still in their shells, to the eggs and tadpoles of other amphibians, and even smaller newts.

The colors and spots of most male newts get bigger and brighter during the breeding season. The crest gets bigger, too, as on this smooth newt. This helps to impress the females, for successful mating.

▼ **Rough-skinned newts** live along the Pacific northwest and have especially horrible skin fluid, which keeps away most predators. During the breeding season, the male's skin loses its tiny bumps and gets very smooth.

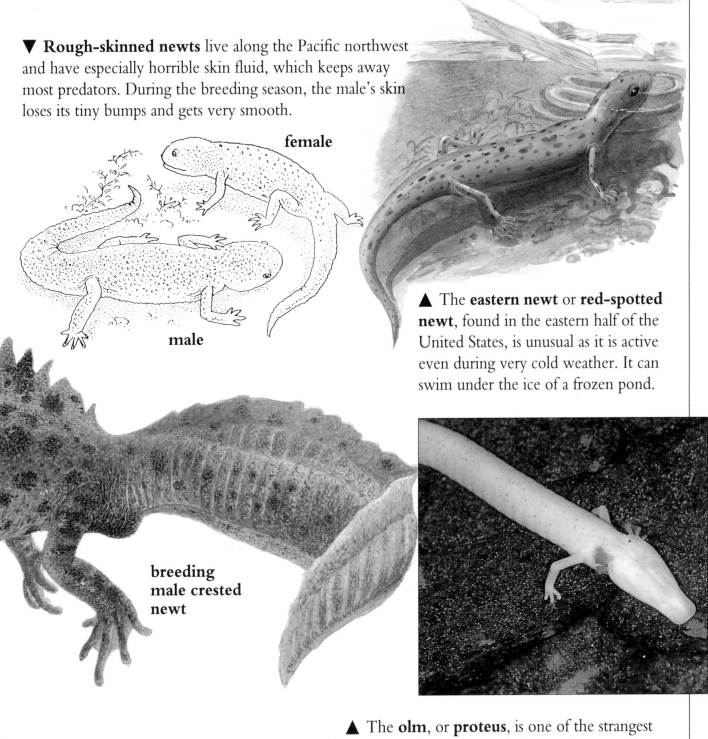

female

male

breeding male crested newt

▲ The **eastern newt** or **red-spotted newt**, found in the eastern half of the United States, is unusual as it is active even during very cold weather. It can swim under the ice of a frozen pond.

▲ Only the male **crested newt** has the wavy-skinned crest on his back. The rest of this newt's skin is dark, slimy and slippery, with warty lumps.

▲ The **olm**, or **proteus**, is one of the strangest members of the newt and salamander group. It grows up to a foot long, and lives only in the underground streams and lakes of the Carpathian Mountains in southeastern Europe. Almost blind, it eats water animals such as shrimps and worms.

Glossary

Amphibian A member of the animal group *Amphibia*, including frogs, toads, newts, salamanders, and caecilians. Amphibian means "two lives" because most amphibians live in water and on land.

Caecilian A type of amphibian with no legs and tiny eyes. It looks like a big earthworm or small snake.

Camouflage Colored and patterned to merge and blend in with the surroundings.

Defense pose Body position and behavior designed to make an animal look big and fearsome, to scare away enemies and predators.

Eggs Small rounded objects, laid by the female, from which the young animals grow. Amphibian eggs, or spawn, are usually dark specks surrounded by see-through jelly.

Eyespots Round colored patches on the body that look like the big eyes of a hawk, cat, or owl. False-eyed frogs and many other animals use them to frighten away predators.

Frog A type of amphibian with a wide mouth, small body, small front legs, very large back legs, no tail, and smooth moist skin. (See **Toad**.)

Gastric-brooder A creature that cares for its young by keeping them in its stomach.

Gills Feathery body parts on an animal that lives in water. The gills are filled with blood, and take in life-giving oxygen from the water, so that the animal can breathe underwater. (See **Oxygen**.)

Lungs Spongy parts inside the body of an animal. Lungs take in air when the animal breathes and transfer life-giving oxygen from the air to the animal's blood. (See **Oxygen**.)

Metamorphosis A change in body shape during the development of an animal. For example, tadpoles change into frogs.

Microscopic Something that is so small, you can see it only by using a microscope (a very powerful kind of magnifying glass).

Newt A type of amphibian with a long slim body, four small legs, and a long tail. Newts are in the salamander group of amphibians.

Oxygen A colorless, invisible gas that makes up one-fifth of the air. Animals need to breathe it to live.

Parotid gland A lumpy part under the skin, behind an animal's eye or near its ear. In a toad, it makes horrible-tasting fluid. In a human, it makes saliva (spit).

Predator An animal that hunts other animals for food, called prey.

Prey A creature that is hunted for food by other animals.

Salamander A type of amphibian with a long slim body, four small legs, and a long tail.

Tadpole A young amphibian, which has a head and tail, but no arms or legs. It is the larva stage of a frog.

Toad An amphibian with a wide mouth, a stout body, small front legs, and generally small back legs, no tail, and a rough, dry skin. (See **Frog**.)

Vocal sac A loose, balloon-like flap of skin that an animal can blow up to make its calls and songs louder.

Warning colors Bright colors and patterns that make an animal easy to see. They warn that the animal is dangerous or tastes horrible.

Index

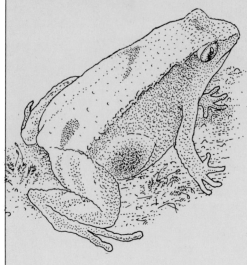

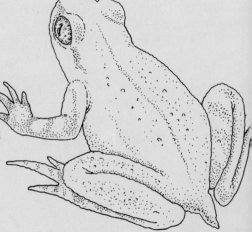

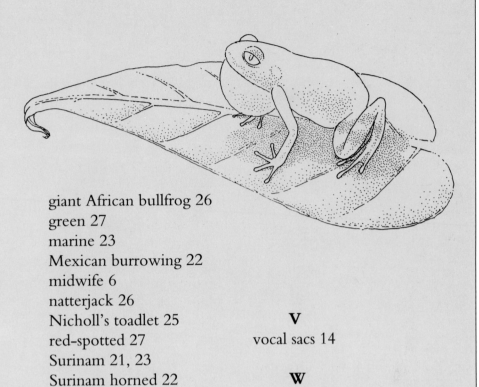

A TEMPLAR BOOK

Devised and produced by The Templar Company plc
Pippbrook Mill, London Road, Dorking,
Surrey RH4 1JE, Great Britain
Copyright © 1993 by The Templar Company plc